Ruth and Boaz

NOT YOUR AVERAGE LOVE STORY

LYNLEY FISHER

Ark House Press
arkhousepress.com

© 2025 Lynley Fisher

Unless otherwise stated, all Scriptures are taken from the New International Translation (Holy Bible. Copyright© 1996, 2004, 2007, 2013 by Tyndale House Foundation. Used by permission of Tyndale House Publishers Inc., Carol Stream, Illinois 60188. All rights reserved.)

Illustrations (excluding map) from Sweet Publishing and FreeBible images.org

Cataloguing in Publication Data:
Title: Ruth and Boaz
ISBN: 978-1-7641051-8-7 (pbk)
Subjects: REL006850 RELIGION / Biblical Studies / Old Testament / Historical Books; REL012030   RELIGION / Christian Living / Family & Relationships; REL074000   RELIGION / Christian Ministry / Pastoral Resources;

Design by initiateagency.com

'May you be richly rewarded by the LORD, the God of Israel, under whose wings you have come to take refuge.'

The Book of Ruth 2:12

CONTENTS

CHAPTER 1

Moab, circa 1100 BC

Although this story will have a happy ending, we begin with a sad image of a grieving family. They are standing at the burial site of their father, Elimelek. He'd been an Israelite from Bethlehem, in Judah country.

Naomi, his widow, held the hands of their two sons, Mahlon and Kilion.

These young men held the hands of their Moabite wives, Ruth and Orpah.

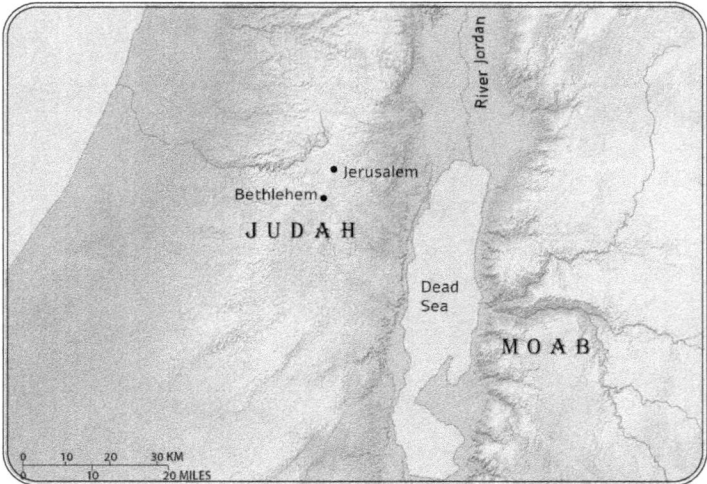

Naomi gripped her sons, afraid her knees would give way. Her tears of grief mingled with regret, resentment and bitterness. Under her breath she moaned, 'My darling Elimelek, see what has happened because we came to Moab – this pagan place? You aren't even being buried with your ancestors.

Oh LORD, why have you taken my husband? Was it to punish us for coming here to Moab?'

Naomi had never felt right about their move away from Judah.

Elimelek had come home so disheartened that day. It was ten years ago now. He'd thrown himself onto the goatskin rug, and to her alarm, began to cry, 'My homeland, my homeland!'

'Naomi,' he said, slowly sitting up, 'I've decided we should leave this place – and soon.'

'What do you mean 'leave'?' she asked, confused.

'Leave Bethlehem, leave Judah, take the boys and move to… to Moab,' Elimelek answered, with a certainty he didn't really have. 'It'll only be for a while – until this famine is over.'

'Moab?' she cried. 'You're not thinking straight, Elimelek. We can't leave our people and our land! It'd be like putting a hole in the very heart of Israel. Not to mention the Moabites have been fighting us since we've been here. They see us Israelites as enemies.'

'All my hope for this land is lost,' Elimelek moaned. 'There's been no kind of leadership since each of our tribes settled on their land. Without a king or any military, people are running amok.

The famine's gone on too long. There's no harvesting and no work. I can't think what else to do. And as for our people! So many have turned from the LORD'S way, it's out of control. I feel like a foreigner in my own land. People here in Judah are fighting each other.'

'Have you prayed about this? Have you been to the priests?' Naomi asked. 'The priests can advise you.'

'The priests themselves throw their hands up and say we are living in a land of 'Humanism, Relativism and Existentialism'.'

'What are they?' she asked, furrowing her brow. The priests were always using too many big words.

Elimelek shrugged. 'I don't know. But they're all bad. People are going by their own rules and doing anything they like. If only we had a king! Then they'd have to follow the law and we could be a happy, united people that the LORD would bless. There'd be no famines.'

Naomi could see that Elimelek had made up his mind and just needed to see a glimmer of hope for his family's well-being. But Moab? Moabites did not follow Jehovah. They worshipped their own pagan gods and she'd heard all about them. There was Baal and his wife Asheroh, and the Moabites believed that when these gods have sexual relations, their land becomes fertile. Their main god sounded so fierce and horrible. His name was Chemosh and he wasn't content with animal sacrifices, he wanted children.

Naomi had not been happy about moving to Moab. If they left Judah—the land the LORD had specifically given to them—were they also leaving the LORD's covering?

Naomi left Elimelek's burial place, her heart aching. He was gone, along with any hope of ever returning home to Judah. The boys had married into Moabite families. She would probably die here too.

CHAPTER 2

The Israelite brothers, Mahlon and Kilion, were dead.

Silence surrounded the three widows, sitting on the goatskin, under a simple bough shelter. They'd been wailing there for days and were now empty and exhausted.

Naomi looked across at Ruth and Orpah, their sweet, tear-stained faces. After Elimelek's death, her boys and their wives had cared for her so well. But now, she was the only Israelite in the village, and no longer had any men to protect her. These pretty young girls would find new husbands quickly and they'd be Moabite men. Who'd want her around? Who'd care for her, provide for her? The only one she could turn to now, was the LORD.

So, Naomi prayed.

Not long after this, a neighbour returned from his travels over to the other side of the Jordan River. Naomi couldn't wait to hear if he had any news of her country.

'The famine over there has finished,' the neighbour told her. 'Actually, their harvest this year is predicted to be so big, I reckon they'll have more than they need.'

Naomi caught him giving his brother a sly wink. She wouldn't put it past these two to be part of a marauding gang that goes over and steals Judah's harvested grain. Back in Bethlehem, Elimelek was constantly trying to outsmart thieves by hiding their harvest.

She politely bid the neighbour goodbye then almost ran back to her daughters–in–law.

'Girls,' she said, more animated than she'd been in months, 'Sit down and listen.'

Knowing that what she was about to say would be a shock, she took a few deep breaths and spoke slowly.

'Now, Ruth and Orpah, we had never intended to stay in Moab forever, you know. Elimelek has a field back home. It's mortgaged of course, and something needs to be done about that, but apparently, the famine–that went on for so long – is now over. God has again turned His face on our people and the Holy Land.

So, I've decided to go back home–to Bethlehem. There is no longer any reason for me to stay here in Moab.' She didn't mention how she hated living among the pagan Moabites. 'I have relatives and friends, and I believe God will bless me for coming back under His Holy covering. We should never have left in the first place. Now, I'm going to take the washing down to the spring and leave you to talk this over.'

The girls saw the hope in Naomi's eyes. They knew how much she pined for the place she called the 'Holy Land'.

'Are we supposed to go too?' Orpah asked Ruth. She'd never left her village. What about her own family?

'We're not really obligated,' Ruth said, 'but we can't let her go back on her own. It would be 80 kilometres to Bethlehem. Naomi is a shadow of what she was, and who knows what she might encounter on the way.'

'But what can we do? I barely have the strength to carry the water skin myself. I'd be no protection.' Orpah trembled at the enormity of the whole idea.

'From Naomi's stories, I think Israel sounds wonderful,' said Ruth, whose life had been so much better since joining Mahlon's beautiful family. 'And their God is kinder. He sounds harsh if he did bring on that famine, but Naomi sings of his mercy and love. There's no love from our gods here—it's just fear. I don't have to think twice. I'm going with her.'

Orpah was not as keen as Ruth to leave her home, but she'd grown to love Ruth as a sister and now felt a duty to support Naomi. She also knew that Naomi and Ruth were the only ones who shared her grief. The three women had become very close.

'Ok. I'll go too.' Then she grinned at Ruth. 'And, we already know how handsome the Israelite men are!'

'Orpah! How can you think of another husband so soon?' Ruth scolded her light–heartedly but was relieved not to lose Orpah.

It didn't take the women long to sort out which belongings they needed to pack – only the barest essentials. Naomi drew a map in the sand for them.

'We'll go back the same way Elimelek brought me and the boys over here,' she said. 'We'll walk up this way, to the north side of the Dead Sea and then cross over here, at the Jordon River. If all goes well, we should be able to make it in five days.

CHAPTER 3

They weren't that far along the way, when Naomi starting having second thoughts about the girls coming with her. She did want them, and needed them. She didn't want to do this journey alone. But was this just being selfish? She knew from first–hand experience how hard it was to be a foreign woman on another's land. What was she leading them into?

'Girls, stop here,' Naomi said, putting down the rolled–up goatskin mat that held her belongings. She wasn't going to leave *that* behind. 'I think you should both turn around and go back home to your families.'

'No way,' they both assured her. 'We're coming back with you.'

Naomi's determination grew. She would rather be in need herself than put her daughters–in–law in any need or trouble.

'Think about it,' she said, now resting on the mat. 'Why come with me? I can't give you another husband. I'm too old for that. If

God's rod is upon me for doing the wrong thing, it has nothing to do with you. I don't want you to have to suffer the consequences of my sin.'

'What do you mean 'sin'? What 'sin'?' Orpah was confused at this change of heart. 'What have you done, Mother?'

"Sin' is simply walking away from the LORD. I don't think He wanted Elimelek and me to leave the land He gave us. This may have been some sort of punishment, and so He has turned His hand against me.

Orpah still didn't understand.

'There are some big words the priests used back home that I still remember,' explained Naomi. 'They would call them 'The 4 big 'R's'. When people are in rebellion against the LORD, you can be sure retribution will come. But if the people sincerely repent of their selfish ways, He promises to restore them and bless them.

So, you can see why I must go home. You have both shown me so much kindness and were good wives to my sons. May the LORD show you the same kindness and may He give you fine husbands, who will love you and keep you safe. Go back to your own mothers' home.'

Both Orpah and Ruth were crying at this.

Orpah was also considering the realities. Naomi was setting her free.

'Oh, my dear, dear, Mother–in–law,' she threw her arms around Naomi and kissed her goodbye.

'You too, Ruth,' Naomi said, as firmly as she could manage. 'Go back with her to your own people.'

Ruth shook her head. Orpah's resolve to continue the trek to Judah had weakened but Ruth's strengthened. She couldn't let Naomi walk alone. She just couldn't. Also, she didn't want to be with people who worshipped other gods. She now knew a little of Naomi's God, Jehovah, and it felt safer to be with Him. She had seen a truth in Naomi's faith and wanted to be part of it.

'Don't push me away,' she pleaded. 'I want to come with you. I want to be with you. You have been more of a mother to me than my own.

Where you go, I will go, and where you stay, I will stay. Your people will be my people and your God, will be my God. Where you die, I will die and there I will be buried.'

Naomi was astounded at the courage of this young girl and the love that shone through her support.

'Come on then,' she said, secretly delighted, 'we still have a few hours of daylight left.'

CHAPTER 4

That first night, Naomi and Ruth found a place to camp behind a group of large rocks. Here they prayed the LORD would keep them safe and unseen.

They built a small fire and Naomi made some flat bread. It was cooking well on the coals and Naomi deftly flipped it over, using no more than her fingertips.

Ruth took a sip from the wine skin.

'Tell me about Bethlehem, Naomi,' she asked, hoping this might lift Naomi's spirits. 'Is it far from the city of Jerusalem? What's it like?'

'Bethlehem is only about 8 kilometres from Jerusalem. It's all terraced. I've told you about our beautiful hills. They're not as high as the hills of Moab, but I used to love to sit up there and look across the valley to the Dead Sea. Moab's over here on the other side. You'll still be able to see your homeland, child.'

She lifted the bread from the fire and dropped it onto a stone to cool. 'I pray your move to this new homeland will go well for you. The LORD promises us, that those who honour their parents will live long and live well. You've honoured me more than I could have hoped from any daughter. So, may this be true for you.' She began to weep.

Ruth lent across and hugged her. 'It's so easy to love you, Naomi. You have always shown me love and support. Come on now, cheer up. We're both starting a new life – a new adventure. You've always spoken so fondly of your Bethlehem. Aren't you happy to be seeing your old friends and relatives?'

'I'm not happy about much at all,' Naomi sniffed. 'Only the LORD knows what awaits us there. I'm sure we'll find shelter with family, but you may have to go out and glean.'

'What's that?' Ruth asked with some alarm, and the most horrible occupations came to mind.

'It's just picking up the bits and pieces left over from harvesting. We have a welfare law in Israel to look after poor people (like us) or foreigners. It's from our Book of Leviticus. The Law requires landowners to tell their harvesters to always leave a section of unharvested crop, so that those in need can take a share. They can also pick up pieces that get dropped or left behind. Don't look so worried,' Naomi said. 'That's what 'gleaning' is. But I don't know if my own back is up for it.'

Over the following days, Ruth grew excited about their destination. She wished Naomi was more positive. They were both still emotionally fragile, but Ruth could see Naomi was finding the journey physically demanding as well. She was ten years younger the last time she came this way.

Only when they could finally see Bethlehem did Naomi smile.

'There! Can you see, Ruth? Can you see how its terraces make it look like a big breadbasket? The Breadbasket of Judah!'

'So *that's* why it's called 'Bethlehem' (House of Bread) said Ruth, pleased to be learning some more. 'Do they also make a lot of bread?'

'No one was making much bread when we left,' Naomi answered, grimly. 'There was famine throughout this whole area and people were starving. There were no wheat crops, so no flour and therefore, no bread. But things are different now, praise the LORD. He's sent the rain and this year's crops are said to be bumper. Bethlehem will again live up to its name.

It's spring harvest time, so our Festival of Shavuot will be on now. It's the anniversary of when the LORD gave us the Law through Moses. The barley harvest will be just starting, so there should be plenty of work. '

Ruth noticed Naomi pulling up her robe and quickening her pace.

By late afternoon they reached Bethlehem and women came running from everywhere.

'Naomi? Is that you?' they cried. They couldn't believe she'd look so different.

She embraced them weeping, 'I am no longer your pleasant Naomi. You may as well call me 'Mara' because my life has turned bitter. I have lost everyone.'

Ruth understood what she meant, but Naomi still had her. She was standing right there. And these Israelite women were acting as if she wasn't. They didn't look at her.

'Elimelek and my sons,' Naomi continued, 'they're all gone. Their bodies resting in a pagan land. The Almighty has turned His face from me!'

The wailing began all over again, as the town received the news that Elimelek's widow had returned *and* she'd brought with her a Moabite teenage girl.

CHAPTER 5

Bethlehem. Circa 1100 BC

Elimelek's dwelling was an empty shell but it provided Naomi and Ruth with somewhere to live. Naomi's friends generously brought her all she needed. When they visited, they eyed Ruth suspiciously and didn't speak to her.

Ruth was grateful for their provision but didn't want to be someone who just takes charity. She was well rested now after their five day trek and wanted to earn her keep and Naomi's too.

'Is it ok, if tomorrow, I go out and try this 'gleaning'?' she asked her mother–in–law.

'Yes,' said Naomi, 'good idea.' She and Ruth had been busy making themselves a little home, but she could see Ruth needed to get out and about. Naomi didn't want to be living on handouts either. 'You won't find it hard to spot the harvesters. There'll be plenty of teams working tomorrow. But do the right thing, Ruth, and first find the 'overseer'–the man in charge. Just ask him if you can glean. Most will say 'yes'. As a foreign girl you're going to have to be polite and keep a low profile. Stay close to the women.'

The next morning, Ruth set out early. After a time, she came across a group carrying sickles. They were heading down a side–track. Assuming they were harvesters off to work, she followed them with her heart thumping.

They came to a field and she saw a man standing at the gate welcoming them all.

'Shalom.'

'Shalom.' They all walked casually through the gate with a greeting and a nod, until Ruth was face to face with the overseer.

'Who are you?' he asked, straightening himself in a business–like manner. He knew who she was. It was a small town.

His change of attitude sent her anxiety levels rising but she had to do what she came to do.

'Sir, I am Ruth. My mother–in–law is Naomi, Elimelek's widow. We arrived here from Moab a couple of days ago. May I please glean in your field?' She kept her eyes downcast and trembled as she spoke.

Ruth's sweet humility touched the overseer's heart. The poor girl sounded like she'd rehearsed her lines. He let her through the gate and pointed to where she should go.

Halfway through the morning, the owner of the field, Boaz, arrived from Bethlehem. He was a big man and smiled to the harvesters who'd all stopped to wave at him.

'The Lord bless you!' he boomed, looking pleased with the progress they were making.

'The Lord bless you!' they called back.

Ruth had seen work teams back in Moab. The bosses weren't usually so friendly with the workers and the language was usually coarse. From up the back, she could see Boaz speaking to this person and that person, obviously just being friendly and asking, 'How are you today?'

Walking around, he eventually noticed Ruth and strode over to the overseer.

'Who's that foreign woman up the back?' Boaz asked.

'She's the Moabite woman who arrived back in town with Naomi,' explained the overseer. 'She came in early this morning and asked me if she could glean. I knew you'd want me to say, 'yes'.'

'Quite right,' Boaz said. He was a wealthy man but not the type to lord it over others. He was also a strong man of God and knew the scriptures well. Boaz's name means 'in Him is strength' and he lived by this name.

Boaz had heard all about Ruth and how she'd been so good to her mother–in–law and accompanied Naomi all the way from Moab–an arduous journey for two women alone. And both recent widows.

He walked down to speak to her.

'Ruth, is it?' Boaz spoke softly, knowing she might be frightened.

'That's right, Sir,' she answered without looking at him directly.

So Boaz said to Ruth, 'My daughter, listen to me. You don't need to go and glean in any other field. Don't go away from here. Stay here with the women who work for me. Just watch the field where the men are harvesting and follow along after the women. I've told the men not to lay a hand on you. And whenever you are thirsty, go and get a drink from the water jars the men have filled.'

Ruth scarcely believed the owner would come over and speak to her.

She bowed down with her face to the ground. She asked him, 'Why have I found such favor in your eyes that you notice me—a foreigner?'

Boaz replied, 'I've been told all about what you have done for your mother–in–law since the death of your husband—how you left your father and mother and homeland and came to live with a people you did not know before. May the LORD repay you for what you have done. May you be richly rewarded by the LORD, the God of Israel, under whose wings you have come to take refuge.'

Who was this beautiful man who spoke pure poetry? Ruth had never heard anyone speak in such a way. He was praying for her!

'May I continue to find favor in your eyes, my lord,' she said. 'You have put me at ease by speaking kindly to your servant – though I do not have the standing of one of your servants.'

Boaz was impressed with this girl. On top of what he'd heard, she'd obviously been working very hard and she spoke with a humility and sweetness that pleased him.

At mealtime all the workers ate together. Ruth went to sit with the women eating quietly. She was so hungry.

She glanced across to where Boaz was sitting and, oh no, he was looking at her!

'Join me,' he beckoned kindly.

Heart thumping again, she walked over to him.

'Sit here,' he said. 'Have some of this bread and dip it in the wine vinegar.'

When Ruth had tried the bread, he offered her some delicious, freshly roasted grain. This she ate with delight and appreciation. She only ate as much as she needed. There was still much work to do, so she didn't want to overeat. This way there'd be some to take home to Naomi.

Boaz watched her and thought to himself how beautiful she was. She had such pretty, white teeth and a gentle smile.

Seeing the harvesters begin to stand, Ruth understood it must be time to go back to work. Turning to Boaz she said, 'Thank you,

Sir. Thank you for your kindness and generous welcome, today.'
He'd been the first person in Bethlehem to treat her so well.

'You're a good girl,' Boaz said, putting his big hand on her shoulder, 'and a hard little worker. You come back tomorrow. We can do with harvesters like you.'

He stood up with her and gave orders to his men.

'Let this girl gather from among the sheaves–yes, that's right–and don't give her a hard time about it. I'd even like you to leave a few stalks on the ground for her.'

'It's your barley,' they said, unsurprised by Boaz's charity to a foreigner–and a Moabite. He was a wealthy man and could well afford to be charitable, but not all wealthy men help the poor. Boaz was a man everyone respected.

Ruth continued to work until the sun went down and then threshed the barley she'd gathered.

She pressed it tight into a sack, because the smaller it was, the easier to carry. It amounted to 13 kilos, so by the time she arrived home, she was red with dust, aching and exhausted.

CHAPTER 6

'So much grain!' Naomi was overjoyed and surprised at such an amount from one day's work.

'I know,' Ruth managed to smile, 'and, I also have this…' She took a woven pouch from her pocket and gave it to Naomi.

Naomi opened the string, looked in and smiled. She put her nose to it and inhaled with pleasure.

'Roasted barley,' she sniffed, 'and so fresh! Blessed be the man who gave you work today. Now sit down daughter, I'll get you a drink, and you can tell me all about it. I praise the LORD every day for you, Ruth.'

Despite, her aches and pains Ruth's entire being warmed to see the joy she'd brought back to Naomi. And there was still more good news to come.

Naomi, nibbling the barley, handed Ruth a drink and joined her on the goatskin mat.

'So, tell me where you ended up. Were they good to you?' Naomi had prayed for Ruth's protection against any rough ways.

'Yes, very good, Naomi!' she assured her. 'None of the women came over and befriended me but everyone was respectful. I didn't have any trouble. In fact, the owner thought I worked so well, he told me I could glean there for the rest of the harvest. So, I have work! Hallelujah!'

Naomi clapped her hands, 'Hallelujah indeed! The LORD is again smiling on us. So, whose field was it? What's the name of this man who thought so highly of you?'

'The owner's name was Boaz,' said Ruth. 'He was lovely – a really big man, long black hair and greying beard…'

'Boaz?' cried Naomi. 'Of all the fields in the area, you found work with Boaz!'

'You know him?' asked Ruth.

Naomi was now dancing with excitement.

'Boaz is a close relative of Elimelek's–and a rich one. He would have been only too happy to take us in, but I didn't want to use Boaz for his wealth. This is much better! That man is such a blessing. Not just to us but our dead as well. He is showing his respect for Elimelek. Dear Boaz, he's never married. None of us could understand why.' She sipped some wine and shook her head saying, 'Of all the fields!'

'Quite a coincidence,' agreed Ruth. Naomi hadn't mentioned Boaz before.

'A 'Godincidence' more likely!' said Naomi nodding with conviction. 'This is wonderful news, daughter. Now you make sure you only go to Boaz's field. We know you'll be safe there–and stay close with the women, because even in Boaz's teams, there'll be a few rough men.'

'Don't worry Naomi,' Ruth said, 'I wouldn't dream of going anywhere else. Everyone shows Boaz respect. They genuinely like their boss. I didn't hear one grumble about him the whole day. And, I didn't hear any cursing–the whole day.'

'There you are,' Naomi said, 'another miracle.'

CHAPTER 7

Ruth worked happily throughout the entire barley harvest. She stayed close by the other women, and if by chance Boaz walked by, he would always give her a little smile and a respectful nod.

Naomi was overflowing with gratitude, for their abundant grain supplies and to have Ruth living with her. How blessed she was to have Ruth. But she knew their situation couldn't go on forever.

She was not the slightest bit interested in marrying again, but it was different for Ruth, still so young. Ruth should have someone looking after her, someone who would love her and protect her and perhaps care for her mother–in–law.

And Naomi knew just where to find him.

'Ruth, come and join me on the mat for bread and wine,' Naomi called. 'We need to talk.'

They now had a small wooden table on the goatskin. Naomi's flatbread was steaming hot and fluffy.

'That smells so good,' said Ruth coming in. 'I hope everything is alright. What do we need to talk about?' She sat down and waited for Naomi to either say something or break the bread.

Naomi pulled off a small section of bread and dipped it in the wine vinegar.

'Ruth,' she said softly, 'do you remember me telling you that Boaz was a close relative to Elimelek?'

'Yes,' said Ruth. She could tell by the way Naomi spoke that something big was coming.

'Here in Israel, Boaz, because he's a close relative, also has the obligation–or the opportunity–to be what we call a 'kinsman–redeemer'. Now, I'll explain what that is. Basically, it's a man who is in the position to help out close relatives in trouble or need.'

'Well, he's certainly been doing that,' said Ruth happily. 'Who knows where I'd have ended up or how we would have fared, if it weren't for Boaz.'

'Yes, that's right. But a kinsman–redeemer can help out his family in many ways,' continued Naomi. 'Say, for example, a family member has had to become a slave to someone to whom he has debts. A kinsman–redeemer can buy him, or her, out of slavery. Also, if a family member has been murdered, it's his duty to make sure the murderer is brought to justice.'

'He sounds like a wonderful relative to have,' said Ruth, 'and from what I've heard about Boaz, he would do all those things.'

'A kinsman—redeemer,' said Naomi, 'can buy back a relative's land that has been mortgaged. Now this is what *we* need, Ruth. We need a Judean man to buy Elimelek's land. We don't want to lose our clan's land to other tribes. Also,' Naomi paused and took Ruth's hand, 'the kinsman—redeemer can marry a childless widow. In doing so, Elimelek's, sorry, the dead relative's name is carried on.'

'Naomi?' Ruth swallowed, realizing what Naomi was suggesting.

'Ruth, dear, it's not just anyone who can be the kinsman—redeemer. Firstly, he has to be a close relative—of the same blood. He also has to be willing. Not everyone wants to take on extra responsibility. And lastly, he has to be able. He has to have the money. If all your other relatives are in debt they can't help you. It has to be someone in credit.'

'You're thinking I should marry Boaz?' Ruth asked, now a little pale.

'It's important to me that you have a good home and are well provided for. You deserve the best, my sweet Ruth, for what you've done for me and my family.' Naomi cradled her arms as if holding a baby and cooed. 'And with Boaz, your first son will carry on the family line of Mahlon and Elimelek. You do like him, don't you?'

'But, at his age, he's obviously never wanted to get married, and why would he want *me* – a Gentile?' Ruth's heart was racing again.

'Who wouldn't want you?' Naomi laughed. 'You're strong and pretty. I've seen the way men look at you. And I wouldn't worry about being a Gentile–not with Boaz. His own mother, Rahab, was a Gentile, but she could see there was a better path, a better land to live in. Just like you. Oh, my Ruth, things are lining up. This is perfect, and, I have an idea.'

Naomi's face was beaming. Ruth couldn't think straight, there were so many considerations going around in her head. She let Naomi talk. Anything could be coming next with Naomi.

'So, do you want to hear my idea?' This was going better than Naomi had expected. Ruth was showing no obvious objection. 'Tonight, Boaz will be celebrating the end of the harvest. They'll be having a big feast down there. Now, I want you to have a wash, anoint yourself with oil–it will make you feel fresh and beautiful. Rake it through your hair then put on your finest clothes. Then,' Naomi took a deep breath, 'I want you to go down to the threshing floor. That's where he'll be tonight after the winnowing.'

'Naomi,' said Ruth shocked, 'that's where *all* the men will be tonight. They'll be staying to guard the grain. No women stay the night.' Had Naomi thought this idea through?

'You won't let anyone see you,' insisted Naomi. 'Find a dark corner to watch from and make sure you see exactly where Boaz lies down.' Naomi tried to read Ruth's face.

'And then?' said Ruth, willing herself to stay calm.

'And then, when they've all finished their feasting and are snoring their heads off, you go over to Boaz,' Naomi said, as if it was obvious.

'*What*!' Ruth asked, 'What are you asking?'

'You go over to Boaz, lift up his robe or blanket and uncover his feet. Lie down there quietly, at his feet. When he wakes up, offer to be his wife.' Naomi held her hands in prayer.

'Let me think about this, Mother,' Ruth said. 'I might go for a walk up the hill. I'll look over to Moab and think about what you've said.'

'That's a good idea,' said Naomi pleasantly, while trying to contain herself. 'I'll get the fire going and the stew on. While you're on the hill, pray to Jehovah. And can you ask our neighbor for a lemon?'

The old lemon tree was full of juicy fruit. Ruth gestured to the woman there. 'May I have one?' The woman nodded then looked back at the dough she was kneading. She didn't want a conversation with the Moabite.

Ruth put the lemon in her pocket and made her way up one of the pretty hills of Bethlehem. She found a spot where she could see across the valley to her homeland. She did miss friends and family, but she had never known such love before coming into Mahlon's family. She'd also never known such grief, but ever since she'd decided to walk with Naomi back to Bethlehem, they'd had many blessings. As Naomi explained, the LORD's face was turned back to them and He had indeed been 'Jehovah Jireh', her provider of safety, shelter and bread.

Following Naomi back to a new land had been risky. Ruth knew there were wild animals and dangerous men out there. Somehow, Naomi's faith in her LORD had made Ruth feel safer. And they were. They survived that journey and did well through the harvest. Ruth had never thought of herself as being a risk taker, but Naomi seemed to think otherwise. As for this 'perfect' idea of hers, there were so many ways it could go horribly wrong.

Boaz was a fine man. Ruth had witnessed his generosity and tenderness many times over the season. Boaz was also a man of principle, a Godly man who would obey the Law. He would be a safe and gentle husband.

When she thought of Mahlon, Ruth knew she'd never have a love like that again – that young, giddy love. She would treasure his memory, but here in Israel, her life and circumstances had completely changed.

She felt a peace about Boaz and it was a peace that surprised her.

On her return, Ruth told Naomi, 'I will do as you suggest.'

Naomi hugged her and cried with joy. She was sure Boaz would do the right thing when he discovered Ruth. He had always been trustworthy and respectful.

CHAPTER 8

Naomi draped a dark shawl over Ruth's head and shoulders while warning her, 'It will be dark in there, Ruth, so be very careful. Keep out of sight and don't look at any of the men. After Boaz has finished eating and drinking, go to where he is, uncover his feet and lie down at them. Remind him he is a kinsman–redeemer of our family. He'll know what you're talking about and will tell you what to do.'

Ruth's faith in Naomi had proved right so far, so she agreed to do exactly as Naomi said – though not without some reservations.

Although it was nearly dark, there were men still winnowing at the door of the barn. As they tossed the barley into the air, the evening breeze caught the chaff and blew it away. The heavier, edible grains fell in a pile on the ground.

Ruth waited behind some bushes until finally the meal was ready and the men went inside. She could hear them, all in good cheer at their supper.

Staying within the shadows, Ruth crept in and found a dark place to hide behind a large pile of kernels. The feast was in the middle of the barn and all the men sat around an array of mouth-watering dishes and small lamps. They were in the light, so Ruth could clearly see Boaz.

He was celebrating. The good years had returned and he praised the LORD. By the time he'd finished his meal and wine, Boaz was in good spirits but very tired. Ruth watched anxiously, waiting for him to lie down. When eventually he did, he walked up to the far end of the pile of grain. This was well away from where the others were bedding down.

It didn't surprise Ruth that they were all asleep within minutes. *This is it*, she thought, and tiptoed around the legs of the exhausted harvesters and up to the end of the pile. She carefully uncovered Boaz's feet and curled up at them like a little turtle dove.

Later that night, something startled Boaz. Turning over, he felt a body at his feet. He sat up quickly. All of the lamps were now out.

'Who's that?' he asked, but without much concern. The body felt more like a child.

'It's me, Ruth,' she whispered nervously.

'Ruth?' Boaz spun back amazed. 'What are you doing here?' he kept his voice low too, but couldn't hide his surprise.

'You are a kinsman–redeemer of our family, Boaz. I've come to ask you to cover me–just with the corner of your garment. Will you cover me, with *your* wings?'

Ruth bent her face to the floor with such humility it pained Boaz's heart.

'This poor, dear girl and all she's been through,' he thought, 'and she's remembered the words I used when we first met.'

'My dear daughter,' he said, gently taking her hand. 'Here, sit up. You are always showing kindness to others. There are other younger and more handsome men you could have gone to–both rich and poor. I am so touched you came to me. Relax now and don't be afraid. I will do what you ask.'

Boaz gave Ruth a smile, of such reassurance – as though he may have already considered this.

'Everyone in Bethlehem now knows you are a woman of the finest character–even if they don't show it,' he said.

Ruth breathed easy once more. Boaz had accepted–just like that. Praise the LORD.

'However,' Boaz continued in a somber tone, 'there is actually another kinsman–redeemer of our family who is more closely related than me.'

'What?' Ruth's heart filled with a sickening dread.

'Look, stay here for the night,' soothed Boaz, 'and tomorrow, I'll go and see him and talk with him about this. If he wants to redeem you, then that's the way it's supposed to be. But if he doesn't, be sure that *I* will. Lie here until morning. You'll be safe until then. I'll sneak you out at daybreak. No one will even know you've been here.

Ruth lay curled up again at Boaz's feet. She didn't sleep at all. There was even more anxiety than earlier. At least she knew Boaz. Was she going to have to be the bride of a man she didn't even know? Why was she constantly leap–frogging into the unknown?

At first light, Boaz stirred and Ruth whispered, 'I should go now, before I'm recognized.'

'Yes, but first give me your shawl,' Boaz said. 'Hold it out for me.' He poured six measures of barley into the shawl, tied it up tight and placed the bundle on her back. 'Don't go home to Naomi empty–handed,' he said, 'and you leave it all to me, sweet Ruth.'

The barley she carried home–another blessing from Boaz–was also his careful protection against what others might think if they saw Ruth out and about so early in the morning.

'Naomi hadn't slept either and was sitting up waiting for her daughter to return. She greeted Ruth with arms outstretched and a hopeful smile.

'Well, are you married?'

Ruth explained all that had happened. Boaz was willing to marry her and redeem the land but it wasn't going to be as straightforward as they'd hoped.

'A woman's life is all about waiting,' Naomi said, embracing Ruth. 'All we can do now is wait. Boaz will be true to his word, Ruth, so try not to worry. The LORD knows what's best for us all. And Boaz will make sure this matter is settled, today.'

Ruth wanted the faith of Naomi.

CHAPTER 9

Boaz left for town straight after breakfast. He tried to think about what he would say to the other kinsman–redeemer and how he'd put it. But he couldn't concentrate on anything – except Ruth. He couldn't stop thinking about her–her beauty and her bravery last night.

When he arrived in Bethlehem, he took a seat at the city gate. This was the men's 'courtroom' as they called it. All their legal proceedings took place there. It was where business meetings were held and news was shared.

In Boaz's hand was the title deed to Naomi's property–a leather–bound scroll sealed with wax. The men were all starting to arrive, one by one. It wasn't long before the very relative he needed to speak to turned up.

'My friend,' Boaz approached him, 'Please, come over and sit down. I need to talk with you about a family matter. And, could I have ten of you elders to also sit in with us.'

Boaz looked around and beckoned various elders. They found their places, after some time of shuffling about. Several claimed bad hearing and wanted to sit closer to the speakers.

Boaz turned his attention to the other kinsman–redeemer.

'Naomi, as you know, has returned from Moab. She is going to sell off Elimelek's land.' Boaz held up the scroll. 'I thought I'd better let you know about this before she does–in case *you* were in a position to buy the land. If you are, you can do the transaction here today, in the presence of our elders. As you are the closest relative, you have first opportunity to redeem the land and I am next in line. Would you like to redeem it?' Boaz came straight to the point.

His relative took no time in answering, 'Yes! I will redeem it.'

'I thought you would!' Boaz said. 'It's a fine property. Oh, by the way, when you redeem this land, you'll take on Elimelek's widow, Naomi, and also Mahlon's young Moabite wife. You'll have to marry her so that Mahlon's name will live on.' Boaz let this sink in.

The other kinsman–redeemer scratched his head.

'That could make things very awkward at home,' he said. 'Also, it could confuse issues with my own estate. I can't redeem it after all. You can buy it yourself, Boaz.' He lowered his head, disappointed, then took off his sandal and gave it to Boaz. This was the way the Israelite men completed any legal transactions regarding the redemption of land.

Boaz turned to the elders and onlookers. Quite a crowd had now gathered.

'Today you are all witnesses that I have bought Elimelek's land from Naomi and have acquired all his property,' he said loudly. 'This includes Ruth, Mahlon's widow. She will be my wife so that his name will live on through his property and the whole town of Bethlehem.'

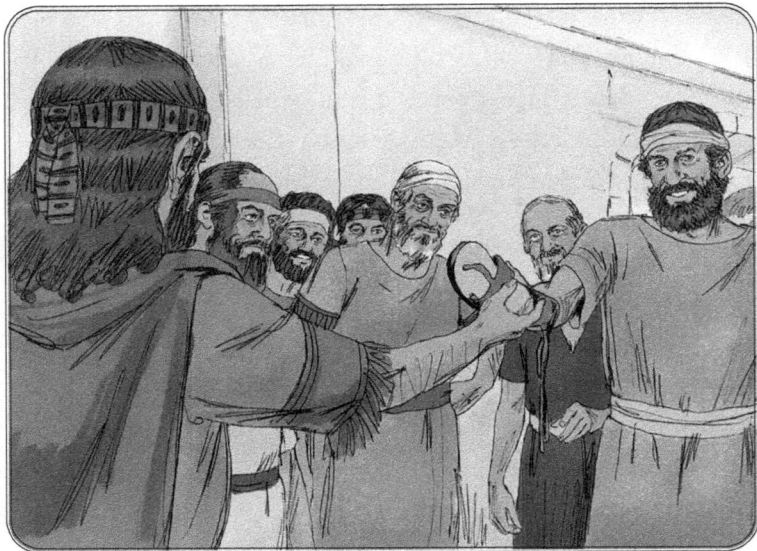

Everyone standing at the gate agreed, 'Yes, we are witnesses,' they called and some sent forth prayers blessing Ruth and Boaz, and the baby they would have.

When Boaz walked up to Naomi's place to tell them the good news, the sky had never been bluer and he'd never felt such a joy in his step.

The two women were waiting outside. Even from a distance Naomi could see the smile on Boaz's face as he waved triumphantly. She pushed Ruth to run to him. 'Go, Girl, go!' she laughed.

Tears of relief trickled down her cheeks as Ruth collapsed into his big arms. He was her husband.

It was not long before Ruth conceived and she gave birth to a son. Naomi's friends were all there and they praised the LORD that she had not been left without a kinsman–redeemer. *'May he become famous throughout Israel,'* they said, 'and may he care for you in your old age, Naomi.'

To Ruth's astonishment the women then added, 'Naomi, you have a daughter–in–law who is better to you than seven sons.' They were finally acknowledging her and even praising her.

As Ruth laid the baby in Naomi's arms, the women began to dance and sing, *'Naomi has a son, Naomi has a son!'*

Her happy bubble of acceptance popped in an instant. Ruth turned to Boaz, her adoring husband, '*Naomi* has a son?' she queried.

Boaz drew her closer, 'You'll get used to them,' he whispered in her ear. 'These women know nothing outside Bethlehem. They're suspicious of the unknown. When they get to know you, they will fall in love with you—as I have.'

Their little boy was named Obed and he did become famous – in Israel and beyond—because he had a son named Jesse who had a son, David, who became the king of Israel.

POST SCRIPT

Where Ruth's story ends, ours begins.

The Scroll of Ruth gives us just a glimpse into one year in the life of a young Moabite girl, living near the close of the Neolithic era. Yet God chose to weave her small, quiet story into His great redemptive narrative.

Still read during Shavuot, the Festival of Weeks, Ruth's story echoes Israel's receiving of the Law and prefigures the coming of King David, her great–grandson, and ultimately, Jesus, the promised Messiah and our kinsman–redeemer.

Through Jesus, our debts are paid. Our past redeemed. And our place in God's story secure.

We may be in the middle of the story now—but the Author has already written the ending.

ABOUT THE AUTHOR

Lynley Fisher is a teacher and writer of educational resources. She lives on the mid-north coast of New South Wales, Australia.